Original title:
Galaxy Grins

Copyright © 2025 Creative Arts Management OÜ
All rights reserved.

Author: Gideon Shaw
ISBN HARDBACK: 978-1-80567-814-4
ISBN PAPERBACK: 978-1-80567-935-6

Starlight Whimsy

Stars twinkle like cheeky sprites,
They giggle and dance through the nights.
Comets dash with a silly flair,
Winking knowingly from their lair.

The moon plays tricks on sleepy eyes,
Casting shadows that waddle and rise.
With laughter echoing far and wide,
The universe joins in on the ride.

Daydreams of the Cosmos

Floating through dreams on a spacey cloud,
Alien jokes make the stardust proud.
Planets spin with delightful grace,
Silly faces in every place.

Shooting stars throw confetti bright,
As they zoom past, a comical sight.
Galactic giggles, a playful tease,
Tickling the void with cosmic ease.

Celestial Smiles

Planets wobble in playful glee,
A cosmic dance for all to see.
Nebulas puff like fluffy pets,
Full of jokes we won't forget.

Saturn's rings spin a silly tune,
While asteroids bop, under the moon.
Every star shines with a cheeky grin,
As if the cosmos knows how to win.

Starlit Laughter

Under the blankets of midnight blue,
Stars tell stories both funny and true.
Meteor showers drop punchlines with flair,
Giggles erupt from the stardust air.

Laughter echoes in the void's embrace,
As planets play tag in a charming race.
The sun cracks jokes with a golden ray,
Brightening up every cosmic play.

Cosmic Comforts

Stars wear socks, oh what a sight,
Comets crack jokes in the night.
Planets bounce in a funny game,
Meteorites giggle, what a frame!

Jupiter dances, oh so wide,
While Saturn twirls with rings of pride.
Neptune chuckles, swaying so free,
In this cosmic circus, we all agree!

Merry Meteors

Meteors race, a speedy show,
Winking and blinking, stars all aglow.
They trip on space dust, stumble, and fall,
Laughter rings out, echoing through all.

With every dash, they wave with glee,
These shooting stars, as fun as can be.
In this vast playground, they leap and spin,
Chasing the giggles, we all jump in!

Jovial Journeys

Rockets zoom with silly hats,
Astronauts dance with fluffy cats.
Galaxies swirl like a merry tune,
As space bunnies hop beneath the moon.

Through stardust trails, the laughter flies,
With joyful cheers that light up the skies.
Each twist and turn, a playful jest,
In this cosmic quest, we feel so blessed!

Radiance of Renown

Stars strutting like they own the night,
Shining so bright, oh what a sight!
Their twinkling giggles, a burst of fun,
In this stellar spotlight, we all run!

Supernovas pop with a playful cheer,
While black holes whisper, "Come over here!"
Galactic shenanigans, oh what a scene,
In this cosmic realm, we laugh and preen!

Twinkling Whimsy

In the night, stars dance and play,
They wink and blink, a cosmic array.
Planets giggle, tumble and spin,
While little moons tease with a cheeky grin.

Cosmic kittens chase asteroids round,
With every leap, they spring from the ground.
Shooting stars play tag in the sky,
Leaving trails of giggles as they fly.

Solar Flare Frolic

A sunny star fell from the bright,
Landed in a field, what a sight!
It rolled and tumbled, lost in cheer,
Chasing its shadow, oh so near.

Lemonade clouds drift in the breeze,
While sunspots tickle the bumblebees.
Solar bubbles bounce up high,
Making all the sunbathers sigh.

Comet's Glee

A comet dashed through the night so spry,
With a glittery tail that seemed to fly.
Chasing rambunctious dreamers below,
Leaving sparkles wherever they go.

Children laughed with an ice cream cone,
Wishing on trails that danced like so.
Shooting sweets across the bright black,
Playful wishes, no joy they lack.

Orbiting Wonders

Around the sun, the planets prance,
In their own little cosmic dance.
Jupiter's belly shakes with delight,
As Saturn spins in sparkly light.

Mars throws a party with Martian cheer,
While Venus sings songs that we all hear.
The moons join in with a joyful jump,
Creating a laughter-filled, cosmic thump.

Cosmic Whispers

In the void where stars reside,
A comet sneezed, a cosmic ride.
Planets giggle, twinkling bright,
Space is filled with pure delight.

Asteroids dance in goofy glee,
Wobbling 'round a starry tree.
Gravity's joke holds firm and tight,
Laughter echoes through the night.

Nebulae of Joy

A cloud of colors swirls and spins,
Where quirky light creates some grins.
Supernovae play peekaboo,
While moons just juggle—who knew?!

Shooting stars exchange sweet winks,
As cosmic coffee spills in drinks.
In this realm, all sense is lost,
Fun is found, no matter the cost.

Radiant Glee

Jovian giants laugh and play,
While tiny moons just theft their way.
A starlit contest, who can shine?
They trade their secrets over time.

Galactic hopscotch in the air,
Silly aliens share their flair.
With glitter bombs and silly hats,
Who knew space could be like that?

Whispering Constellations

Triangles laugh, circles collide,
In this space where fun won't hide.
Stars play poker with comets bold,
Trading secrets of old, untold.

Sirius giggles, Vega sings,
Filling the void with joyful things.
In the cosmos, silly pranks reign,
Witty whispers, a happy chain.

Euphoria Amidst the Stars

Among the stars, the laughter flies,
Cosmic jokes and gleaming sighs.
Alien giggles in the night air,
Dancing comets, without a care.

Meteor showers with punchlines bright,
Asteroids chuckle in their flight.
Planets spin with giddy grace,
Tickled by the vastness of space.

Aurora of Amusement

A swirl of colors, silly and bold,
With stories of laughter and joy retold.
Shooting stars wink in playful glee,
As gravity pulls a cosmic spree.

In this vibrant sky, the fun begins,
Where every twinkle hides silly sins.
Galactic giggles, like bubbles they rise,
Spreading delight, like a sweet surprise.

Starlight Secrets

Beneath the moon's soft, glowing face,
Twinkling secrets of time and space.
Whispers of stars on a breezy night,
Sharing laughs with a wink of light.

Nebulas chuckle in hues so bright,
Creating joy in the still of night.
Astrological puns float on by,
While stardust sprinkles the cotton sky.

Illuminated Mirth

In cosmic corners, jokes unfold,
As radiant worlds gather, bold.
Supernova laughs burst forth with cheer,
Echoing merriment far and near.

Galaxies giggle, spinning a tale,
While playful moons craft a lighthearted trail.
The universe chuckles, can't help but grin,
In this grand show, the fun's about to begin.

Infinite Delights

Stars laughing in the night,
Joking with the moon's soft light.
A comet trips on cosmic air,
While aliens play truth or dare.

Planets round in playful chase,
Orbiting with a silly face.
Meteor showers sprinkle cheer,
Bubbles of joy, they disappear.

Nebulae of Happiness

Twinkling wishes drifting wide,
Cosmic jesters take a ride.
In the clouds, they spin and loom,
Painting smiles that chase the gloom.

Galactic pies float on soft beams,
Sliced with laughter, sprinkled dreams.
Floating friends in silly hats,
Dancing light with friendly cats.

Radiant Reveries

Winking stars play peek-a-boo,
Dancing shadows, bright and new.
Nighttime whispers tickle ears,
As giggles burst like tiny spheres.

Rockets zoom with giggly glee,
Chasing laughter through the sea.
Spinning moons take silly bows,
With sparkling crowns and crazy cows.

Constellation Giggles

Orion's belt has fashion flair,
Falling stars flip through the air.
Cosmic puns float in the void,
Creating joy that won't be toyed.

Sunbeams tickle every face,
As stardust sprinkles all the space.
In the night, we laugh and toss,
With comets playing hopscotch gloss.

Cosmic Canvas of Joy

Stars munch on cookies, oh so bright,
Comets giggle, oh what a sight!
Planets play hide and seek in space,
With moonbeams lighting up the race.

Meteor showers drop confetti trails,
Space critters dance, tell funny tales.
Nebulas swirl in a colorful glee,
Painting the cosmos, wild and free.

Playful Pulsars

Pulsars blink like winking eyes,
Sending out jokes, a cosmic surprise.
With every pulse, they tickle our ears,
Bursting our bubbles, igniting our cheers.

Dancing on quarks, they jiggle and spin,
Creating laughter from deep within.
Their rhythmic beats, a comical tune,
Bringing smiles to all under the moon.

Bubbly Black Holes

Black holes giggle, stretch and yawn,
Swallowing stars, then float till dawn.
They burp out light with a bubbly sound,
Causing a ruckus all around.

With each big gulp, galaxies spin,
Wondering how they'll fit those in.
Creating chaos, but all in fun,
In the cosmic circus, they've just begun.

Celestial Harmony

Shooting stars play the sweetest chords,
Composing tunes with cosmic boards.
The Milky Way sings a cheeky song,
While asteroids dance, they can't go wrong.

In this stellar choir of merry delight,
Laughter and music fill up the night.
Where laughter echoes through the skies,
And every twinkle is a surprise!

Zenith of Laughter

In a realm where comets play,
The stars dance night and day.
With twinkling eyes and goofy grins,
The universe chuckles, it spins.

Planets in a playful race,
Chasing each other in space.
Meteor showers filled with glee,
What a sight for you and me!

A black hole is a massive joke,
Swallowing laughs, oh what a poke!
Galactic giggles echo wide,
In this cosmic fun-filled ride.

Nebulas in colors bright,
Tickle our funny bones each night.
Infinity bursts with wide delight,
As we share this joy in flight.

Cosmic Chortles

Beyond the stars, a quirky scene,
Saturn's rings are made of green.
With laughter bouncing off the moons,
And silly stardust in our tunes.

Comets crack jokes on their way,
While asteroids dance, come what may.
A playful waltz through space and time,
Where even the vacuum feels sublime.

Shooting stars with pranks to share,
Wishing well with an utmost flair.
Galaxies spin with raucous cheer,
As space-time folds—a surprise near.

Planets giggle, what a sight!
In this universe of pure delight.
With cosmic chortles filling the night,
Let's laugh together, hold on tight!

Whirlwind of Smiles

In a nebula of joy so bright,
Winks from stars, oh what a sight!
The sun yawned wide, let out a grin,
And planets all joined in, let's spin!

Zooming through this vibrant scheme,
Asteroids joining in the dream.
Comets swing by with a shout,
In this whirlwind, there's no doubt.

Saturn's puzzled rings take a spin,
Each giggle a spark from within.
Joy whispers through the cosmic flow,
As laughter seeds the stardust glow.

Twinkling lights are our delight,
Shooting joy into the night.
With each loop, we gather smiles,
In this whirlwind that stretches for miles.

The Light We Share

In the cosmos where quirks ignite,
Jupiter's bounce is pure delight.
With every twinkle from afar,
We shine together, just like stars.

A comet leaps, it takes a dive,
Spreading cheer, we feel alive.
A cosmic party, jumps abound,
With every laugh, we're joy unbound.

Through the cosmos, we float with ease,
Cackling like children in the breeze.
Celestial silliness fills the air,
In every beam, the light we share.

Galactic giggles intertwine,
As we traverse this joyful line.
With every pulse, our hearts align,
In this celestial realm, we shine.

Starry-Eyed Happiness

Under twinkling lights, we laugh and play,
Chasing dreams that dance and sway.
With a wink from a comet, we take a spin,
On a merry-go-round made of starlit skin.

Giggling meteors zoom overhead,
Painting laughter, bright as bread.
Each chuckle bursts like a supernova,
In a universe of joy, we spin and hover.

Whimsical Whirlwinds

In a playful breeze, we frolic wild,
Bouncing like planets, a giddy child.
Jupiter jests with a jovial grin,
While Saturn's rings spin us into a din.

Each star tickles, a cosmic tease,
As we twirl and swirl with perfect ease.
Giggles echo through the night,
In a whirl of colors, oh what a sight!

Cosmic Revelries

Come gather round for a cosmic feast,
Where laughter flows, and joy won't cease.
Asteroids leap with playful glee,
Inviting all to join the spree.

With cupcakes shaped like moons and stars,
We'll dance silly beneath the bars.
A chocolate comet, a jelly filled sun,
In this delightful realm, we've just begun.

Celestial Jests

On fluffy clouds, we joke and jest,
Even the stars can't help but rest.
A dancing sun with sunglasses cool,
Makes even the milky way giggle like a fool.

Time zips by in a joyful race,
As we tumble through this merry space.
With laughter bouncing off each sphere,
In this joyful void, we persevere.

Orbiting Euphoria

In the cosmic cafe, stars sip tea,
Comets juggle with a glee,
Satellites chuckle, orbiting round,
Laughter echoes in space profound.

A moon wearing shades, struts with flair,
Planets play tag in celestial air,
Nebulae howl with joy so bright,
The cosmos dances into the night.

Asteroids toss jokes like confetti,
Black holes spin tales, oh so zesty,
A toaster breaks out in a waltz,
While meteorites prance without faults.

Galactic giggles ring ever clear,
Cosmic clowns tickle the atmosphere,
Stardust sprinkles on grinning faces,
In this space of fun and embraces.

Astral Amusement

Stars in pajamas, ready to play,
Jokes about gravity floating away,
Quasars pull pranks on passing ships,
Even the black holes crack silly quips.

Space mice dance on the rings of a queen,
Making a racket, a hilarious scene,
Rockets burst laughter, fuel up with cheer,
Cosmic confetti showers, oh dear!

Galaxies giggle when comets collide,
Fluffy clouds snicker and take a ride,
With each twinkle and shine, jokes unfold,
The universe plays, fun never gets old.

Cosmic balloons float high in delight,
Planets play charades all through the night,
Laughter returns like a boomerang,
In the space carnival, the fun's never tang!

Celestial Chuckles

The sun wears sunglasses, so chic and bright,
Telling jokes to the stars at night,
Little meteors giggle and rhyme,
While Saturn's rings sway to the chime.

An alien chef flips pancakes in space,
With whipped cream smiles, just in case,
Starfish around the table do cheer,
Who knew the cosmos held such good beer?

Dancing galaxies spin with delight,
Cracking up under twinkling light,
Cosmic laughter fills the vast sphere,
As milky ways spin tales to endear.

With a wink and a nudge, the comets unite,
Making odd shapes, what a sight!
Interstellar jesters with jokes so divine,
Make the universe chuckle, oh how they shine!

Stellar Grins

Asteroids play hide and seek in a whirl,
Distant stars toss confetti and twirl,
Comets skedaddle, leaving a trace,
While the big dipper giggles in space.

A star goes 'ping' like a cosmic bell,
Black holes smile, casting a spell,
Twinkling wishes dance on the breeze,
As planets prattle with cosmic ease.

In the twilight of dusk, space critters hum,
Telling tall tales, how silly they come,
Constellations crack up, wiring the fun,
While stardust sparks brighten the run.

A blurry moon trips on a shooting star,
Saying, "Hey buddy, you've gone too far!"
The cosmos roars with laughter and cheer,
Where every giggle lasts through the year.

Interstellar Joyrides

Zooming through the starry skies,
Wobbly ships with goofy sighs.
Aliens dancing on cosmic lanes,
Laughing hard, avoiding pains.

Asteroids bouncing like a ball,
Purple polka dots, big and small.
With every turn, a silly spin,
Who knew space could be such a win?

Miracles in the Milky Way

Silly comets racing past,
Winking stars make wishes last.
Space squirrels in zany hats,
Juggling cheese with dancing cats.

Floating rocks with funny faces,
Sneezes cause hilarious races.
In this realm of cosmic cheer,
Laughter floats from ear to ear.

Patterns of Playfulness

Galaxy kittens chasing beams,
Bouncing high on starlit dreams.
Quirky planets spinning round,
With giggles erupting sound.

Shooting stars form silly shapes,
Drawing smiles with funny tapes.
Wobbly moons make odd ballet,
Inviting all to laugh and play.

Hopes in Orbit

Floating dreams in fluffy clouds,
Brightly beaming, never loud.
Space jellybeans bouncing high,
Filling hearts with sweet supply.

With every twist and silly jump,
Galactic joy is quite the thump.
Hopes are spinning like a top,
In this fun, we'll never stop!

Hallowed Horizons

In the vastness of deep space,
Where aliens giggle and race,
A comet sneezes with flair,
Leaving stardust in the air.

The moons play leapfrog by night,
While stars twinkle with delight,
Asteroids dance, hats on their heads,
Juggling planets, earning their breads.

The black holes call out with cheer,
Inviting all friends to ad-lib here,
With space mice plotting a prank,
They steal moon cheese, never to thank.

In this playground of light and sound,
Where laughter echoes all around,
Cosmic jokes fill the cosmic void,
In a universe where fun's enjoyed.

Light Years of Laughter

Rocket ships race through the haze,
With engines that giggle and blaze,
They break into laughter, oh so loud,
As aliens gather, a quirky crowd.

Saturn's rings wobble with glee,
Spinning tunes from a cosmic spree,
Planets spin stories with gags,
While space owls hoot, waving their rags.

Galactic jesters flip and twirl,
Chasing comets in a whirlwind swirl,
Shooting stars make wishes with style,
As they wink and dance for a while.

In every corner of the wide expanse,
Jokes drift through the stars in a dance,
Soaring high, let the chuckles begin,
In this universe, joy's never thin.

Jupiter's Jests

On Jupiter's moons, a ruckus brews,
With aliens telling their best news,
A giant storm swirls with a giggle,
While space-time does a silly wiggle.

Galilean friends start to race,
Chasing laughter in a dizzying place,
With moon jellybeans bouncing around,
Creating sweet chaos that knows no bound.

A swirling clown pulls a funny plight,
Making Saturn's rings burst into light,
With space piñatas that burst with cheer,
Candy comets fly far and near.

From the gas giant's warm embrace,
Comes a tickle that lights up the space,
As laughter echoes, lives intertwine,
In a joyous cosmos where all can shine.

Joyful Nebulae

In clouds of colors, bright and bold,
Space critters gather, adventures unfold,
With neon giggles that twist and sway,
Painting laughter across the Milky Way.

Starry fireworks pop and crack,
Creating echoes, leaving no lack,
Space kittens ride on rockets so high,
Chasing rainbows through a painted sky.

In cosmic fairs, they sell silly hats,
To Martian mice and jumping cats,
With giggling globes bouncing round,
In joyful harmony, happiness found.

Through whimsical nebulae, fun takes flight,
Where every twinkle tells of delight,
In this universe of endless play,
Laughter reigns in the starlit ballet.

Enchanted Astra

Stars twinkle like bells, in a cosmic show,
Where space critters giggle, putting on a glow.
Nebulas swirl, like cotton candy at a fair,
With friendly aliens dancing, without any care.

Comets zoom by, with a wink and a beam,
Creating trails of laughter, a sparkling dream.
Planets play hide and seek, behind the sun's rays,
As stardust tickles comet tails, in joyful plays.

Dances of Delight

Little moons hop, like bunnies in flight,
While meteors race, painting trails of light.
In the vast cosmos, laughter fills the air,
Gravity does a jig, without a single care.

Supernovas burst, like fireworks galore,
Leaving behind giggles that echo evermore.
Star clusters twirl, in a merry old spin,
Inviting all planets to join in their grin.

Smiles in the Cosmos

Asteroids chuckle, as they pass by with glee,
Joking with comets, 'Is that a moon or a bee?'
The Milky Way's cheeky, with a wink of bright light,
As Jovian giants giggle, through the velvet night.

Witty little quasars, playing peekaboo,
For every cosmic riddle, there's a grin shining through.
Black holes whisper jokes, with a twist and a fun,
While starlight's laughter dances, under the sun.

Interstellar Happiness

From the edges of space, joy rides the breeze,
With pulsars pulsating, putting minds at ease.
Rockets doing flips, in a cosmic ballet,
While aliens cheer, "Join us, hip-hip-hooray!"

In the void of the night, jests are exchanged,
As weird space creatures showcase their range.
Supernova confetti bursts in a flare,
Celebrating the silly, with unmatchable flair.

Joyful Journeys

In the vastness where stars play,
Space whales dance without delay.
A rocket ship made out of cheese,
Zooms through the cosmos with joyous ease.

Nebulas giggle in vibrant hues,
While quirky aliens sing silly blues.
With comets that twirl and skaters so bright,
The universe sparkles with pure delight.

Planets are having a jolly old tea,
With asteroids bouncing as wild as can be.
Lunar laughs echo, an echoing chime,
In this frolicsome realm, we lose track of time.

A Merry Milky Way

In the Milky Way, where wonders collide,
Jupiter's moons decide to slide.
A party of stars, they giggle in rings,
As Saturn's bright halo adds to their flings.

Shooting stars tumble down with a grin,
Proposing a dance that's bound to begin.
Space dust tickles the tips of our toes,
And laughter erupts where the stardust now flows.

Rocket raccoons hover just near,
Playing sweet tunes for those who can hear.
While Venus plays hopscotch with glee,
Each bounce holds a hint of light-hearted spree.

Comet's Cheer

Comet's tail sways in the dark,
Leaving behind a colorful mark.
It zips by with a chortle so loud,
Waving hello to the nearest cloud.

In orbits of joy, the laughter does twirl,
As meteors dash and around us swirl.
A jovial dance in the space-time glow,
Creating a symphony, a cosmic show.

Every twinkle's a wink from afar,
Each supernova a radiant star.
With sprightly laughter bouncing on high,
In this glittery realm, we learn how to fly.

Laughter Across the Cosmos

Across the cosmos, where tickles reside,
Giggles echo with celestial pride.
A starlit parade with planets in tow,
Chasing comets that spark and glow.

Asteroids jive in a cheeky conga,
While cosmic kittens prance like a mamba.
With jokes spun from solar winds high,
They twirl through the void, oh me, oh my!

When black holes chuckle, what a sight to see,
Each belly laugh spinning in gravity.
Stars burst with laughter, bright as the sun,
In a universe painted with playful fun.

Spacetime Serenade

In a rocket made of candy, we race,
To distant stars with zany grace.
Alien ducks play cosmic chase,
And giggles echo in this wild space.

With marshmallow moons and chocolate beams,
We surf on stardust, living dreams.
Asteroids bounce like silly themes,
And laughter bursts like joyful screams.

The universe winks, a cheeky show,
Quasars twirl in a dizzy flow.
Comets jest, with a joyful glow,
In this cosmic circus, we steal the show.

So pack your jokes and leave your frowns,
For here in orbit, fun abounds.
With every wobble, laughter resounds,
In this serenade, joy knows no bounds.

Eternal Glee

A nebula draped in giggles bright,
Twinkling stars but a playful sight.
Cosmic clowns dance under night,
  As planets spin, they take flight.

Silly voices from the dark,
  Comets hiss and leave a mark.
Over moons, we run and lark,
  With joy that ignites a spark.

Every asteroid brings a pun,
  Rocket rides are simply fun.
In the vacuum, we've just begun,
To laugh until we've come undone.

So join this jest in cosmic spree,
Where humor reigns, completely free.
Once in infinity, let it be,
A dream of laughter, our decree!

Positive Vortex

In a whirl of colors, twinkling bright,
We spin around in pure delight.
The cosmos giggles, what a sight,
As we bounce through space, hearts light.

Black holes belch like big balloons,
While planets hum our favorite tunes.
Jupiter's rings, they giggle and swoon,
In this vibrant dance beneath the moons.

Space-time tickles, a wondrous game,
Every warp and twist is never the same.
In this swirling joy, we stake our claim,
As laughter echoes, wild and untame.

So ride the waves of the cosmic cheer,
Let your worries disappear.
In this vortex, loud and clear,
The sound of giggles draws us near.

Lightyears of Laughter

From here to there, with silly sights,
We journey far on funky nights.
With every laugh, the void ignites,
As we dance among the starlit heights.

Shooting stars with chicken wings,
Glittering comets bring us flings.
Planetary pranks, and oh what swings,
In this madcap world, joy sings.

Echoes of laughter through the vast,
Tickling our souls, memories cast.
In this cosmic skit, we're unsurpassed,
As hilarity flies, a colorful blast.

So come along, let's drift and spin,
As laughter fills the space we're in.
In the universe's wide-open grin,
We find the joy, where fun begins.

Harmony in the Heavens

In the night sky, stars giggle bright,
Twinkling tales of comets in flight.
Planets play tag, with moons in tow,
A cosmic dance, a silly show.

Asteroids bounce like kids at play,
Flinging rocks to brighten the day.
Uranus winks in a jovial haze,
While Saturn spins in a ringed daze.

Nebulas puff like candy floss,
Colors swirling, oh what a toss!
Galactic clowns with luminescent grace,
In this vast, silly cosmic space.

Hilarity reigns on this starry stage,
Where laughter echoes, and joys engage.
With every burst of supernova light,
The heavens giggle throughout the night.

Mirage of Mirth

A shimmering wink from a distant star,
Whispers of joy travel from afar.
Umbrellas made of stardust gleam,
Scattering laughter, like a happy dream.

Cosmic jesters with tails of light,
Play peek-a-boo in the velvet night.
Asteroid fields — a wild game of leap,
Tickling comets, making them peep.

Bubbles of laughter in a timeless sea,
Floating on laughter, wild and free.
Solar flares sparkle like confetti in flight,
Celebrating fun in the still of the night.

A mirage so sweet in the dark expanse,
Inviting all to join in the dance.
Sparkling moments in this cosmic mirth,
Celebrating the silliness of the earth.

Luminescent Revels

When dusk settles and the lights come out,
Stars throw parties, there's no doubt.
Galaxies swirl like friends on the floor,
In luminous revels, they always want more.

Meteors shower in comedic flares,
Zipping about, lighthearted dares.
Dancing between the wonders of night,
Their cheerful antics are quite a sight.

Waving arms of bright solar winds,
As planets laugh and do silly spins.
Twirling and whirling in bold delight,
This joyousness sparkles, pure and bright.

With every flash, the universe beams,
Crafting a quilt from whimsical dreams.
In their merriment, they play and tease,
In the fabric of time, laughter's the breeze.

The Comet's Smile

A comet zooms with a cheeky grin,
Trailing joy from where it's been.
With a swish of its tail, it tickles the moon,
Making the night sing a happy tune.

Its laughter echoes through the starry vale,
As luminous beings join the trail.
Celestial buddies in unscripted glee,
Igniting smiles, wild and free.

Planetary giggles shake the air,
As meteors tumble without a care.
The universe chuckles, a merry dance,
In the grand spectacle, all take a chance.

A comet's escapades spread joy afar,
As if the cosmos plays on a guitar.
In starlit nights, everyone's in style,
Captured forever in the comet's smile.

Playful Planets

Little Mercury zips around,
Dancing fast, never gets found.
Venus winks with a twinkling eye,
While Mars laughs as he floats by.

Jupiter spins with a great big grin,
Swirling storms that make him spin.
Saturn's rings jingle with delight,
He shows off to the stars each night.

Uranus rolls with a silly face,
Tumbling through the cosmic space.
Neptune chuckles in a blue hue,
Saying, "Hey there, how do you do?"

The comets giggle as they race,
Chasing through the starry place.
Each planet plays a silly game,
In the universe, they all know fame.

Hilarity of the Heavens

Silly stars twinkle 'round the night,
Sharing jokes that feel just right.
Constellations fold in laughter,
As the Milky Way joins after.

The sun shines bright, a golden grin,
Spreading joy to all within.
While the moon, a glowing tease,
Giggles softly with the breeze.

Asteroids tumble, bumping in bliss,
Each big rock wants a funny kiss.
Neon nebulae twist and sway,
Crafting chuckles in their own way.

Planets prance in a cosmic dance,
Every spin is a funny chance.
The heavens burst with playful cheer,
Laughter echoing far and near.

Euphoric Expanses

Beyond the stars, the giggles ring,
Planets chat over moonlit bling.
Cosmic dust shakes with delight,
As galaxies twirl into the night.

Each comet shares a laugh so sweet,
As they zoom and bounce with fleet.
A supernova's joke is loud,
As it bursts forth, drawing a crowd.

Neutron stars play hide and seek,
Twinkling bright while galaxies peek.
The vast expanse is full of cheer,
Echoing laughter, far and near.

Black holes grin with a nighty twist,
Pulling in all, they can't resist.
In the euphoric skies of glee,
Each cosmic joke's a mystery.

Celestial Curiosities

Shooting stars with smiles abound,
Whisper secrets, light the ground.
Galaxies swirl in comic display,
Tickling space in a playful way.

Alien creatures wave and sing,
Dressed in costumes, what a fling!
The planets chuckle at their style,
As they dance across the cosmic mile.

Satellites laugh as they spin around,
Sending signals with silly sound.
Meteor showers sprinkle the night,
Filling the void with pure delight.

With every twinkling spark above,
Heavenly bodies show the love.
In this vast and curious sea,
Laughter floats around so free.

Enigmas of Elation

Stars twinkle like cheeky sprites,
They wink and giggle in the night.
Planets dance in silly hurries,
While comets zoom amid the flurries.

Asteroids play catch with the moon,
Making music with a silly tune.
Jupiter jests, wearing rings too wide,
In this cosmic circus, there's no place to hide.

Nebulae swirl in cotton candy hues,
While black holes hide, feigning snooze.
Whispers and chuckles float in the air,
As galaxies spin in a merry affair.

A rocket ship sneezes, a blast of fun,
As Martians dance beneath the sun.
Alien laughter echoes through space,
In this wild, joyous, cosmic place.

Cosmic Carousels

Round and round, the planets twirl,
In a dance of giggles, they swirl.
Saturn's rings are a merry go-round,
With playful antics, joyfully found.

Silly meteors race without a care,
While Venus shows off her fluffy hair.
Galactic swings, oh what a ride,
As laughter fills the starry tide.

Mars cracks jokes that keep us grinning,
As cosmic games feel just like winning.
Stars bounce like balls in playful flare,
Creating a ruckus in the midnight air.

Patterns of light draw a funny face,
As comets dash in a wild chase.
With each spin, the universe beams,
In this whimsical dance of dreams.

Wondrous Whispers

Whispers of joy twinkle overhead,
As laughter echoes in the bedspread.
Stars share secrets in playful songs,
As the universe hums along.

Planets giggle with each soft breeze,
Comets race in mischievous tease.
In the void, silly sounds collide,
Bouncing off suns, far and wide.

Nebulas gossip with swirling flair,
While asteroids roll without a care.
The cosmos chuckles, a magical jest,
In the arms of the night, we jest and rest.

A supernova bursts into glee,
Lighting up space with jubilee.
In this heaven where joy is spun,
Every laugh is a shining sun.

Elation in the Ether

In the vacuum, a cow jumps high,
Waving at planets as they fly by.
With every leap, a comet grins,
And even black holes spin with whimsy wins.

Asteroids dance in a cha-cha parade,
Creating a ruckus, oh what a charade!
Saturn's rings twinkle, a mischievous wink,
While Martians sip tea and start to think.

Humor of the Stars

Stars stand in line for a cosmic show,
Winking and blinking, putting on a glow.
They tell silly jokes to the moons up high,
As meteorites giggle and zippingly fly.

Planets toss jokes like a juggler's ball,
Echoing laughter through the vast hall.
Orbits twist into puns and delight,
As laughter erupts in the shimmering night.

Nebulous Nuances

In the mist of the void, a joke takes flight,
Dancing with stardust, oh what a sight!
Wormholes play peek-a-boo with a grin,
While cosmic winds hum with a silly spin.

Astro-bunnies hop on a rainbow beam,
Catching moonbeams in a glimmering dream.
Each twinkle of light sparks a hearty laugh,
As space joins in a quirky autograph.

Sparkling Vitality

Shooting stars on a sugar-fueled spree,
Whirling in laughter like children set free.
Planets chuckle in harmonious glee,
Their rings rolling 'round like a cosmic jubilee.

Nebulas swirl in a colorful jest,
Wearing a crown of stars, they feel blessed.
In laughter, the universe finds its refrain,
A joyful embrace in the cosmic domain.

Starlit Smiles

In the night, stars play tricks,
Winking gently, like cheeky picks.
They twinkle bright with silly grins,
Shining down where the fun begins.

Planets spin with a goofy dance,
Galactic pranks in a swirling trance.
Comets whip by, leaving trails of glee,
Laughing softly as they race free.

Nebulas puff in a cotton candy mist,
Whispering jokes that can't be missed.
Supernovae burst, but just for laughs,
Creating fireworks in cosmic quaffs.

In this vastness where humor thrives,
Every light in the sky contrives.
With celestial chuckles, we find delight,
As laughter echoes through the night.

Cosmic Laughter

In the void, where the planets jest,
A black hole sighs, it needs a rest.
Stars mug for the cameras up high,
With cosmic tales that make us cry.

Asteroids tumble, doing ballet,
Through the cosmos, they frolic and play.
A shooting star trips on its tail,
Leaving behind a gleeful trail.

Alien creatures in their odd attire,
Tell us jokes that never tire.
Galactic giggles spread far and wide,
Bringing light to the cosmic tide.

With each orbit, the humor spins,
In this expanse where joy begins.
As we gaze at the velvet night,
The universe chuckles, what a sight!

Celestial Joys

Bubbles of stardust rise and fizz,
Each tickle of light is pure bliss.
The sun grins wide, warming the crowd,
While the moon beams down, softly loud.

Space squirrels chase meteorite nuts,
While galactic kittens roll in ruts.
Jupiter's rings, a merry-go-round,
Puppy stars barking in joy, unbound.

Distant worlds hold their own sing-alongs,
Harmonizing in delightful songs.
Wherever we look, joy blooms bright,
In the cosmos, laughter takes flight.

With comets as pals, we dance through the night,
In this timeless place of pure delight.
So smile with the stars, let worries go,
In the celestial theater, laughter flows.

Luminous Whispers

Whispers of light dance through the air,
Tickling comets with flair and care.
Shooting stars giggle, leaving a trace,
As constellations make funny faces.

Planets tease, each one a prank,
Making the moon, a silver tank.
Galaxies spin, a carousel of fun,
Rolling through space, just like a run.

Astro-dogs bark at the cosmic show,
Chasing the meteors, to and fro.
With laughter echoed in the void's embrace,
Life's a joke in this vast, bright space.

So come join the fun, don't miss the cue,
In this boundless playground, joy's never few.
With each luminous flash, giggles ignite,
A celestial party, under the night.

Brighter Than Stars

In a realm where winks abound,
Laughter echoes 'round and round,
Comets chuckle as they fly,
Jokes are stitched in cosmic pie.

Planets dance with silly cheer,
While moons wear hats, oh so dear,
Meteor showers laugh aloud,
In this scene, we're all so proud.

Galactic pranks on every side,
Asteroids take us for a ride,
With each twirl, a twist of fate,
Punchlines hidden, can't be late.

So raise a toast to skies so bright,
Where humor glimmers in the night,
In this vast and wondrous scheme,
We find our joy; we chase the dream.

Milky Way Mirth

Amidst the stars, a party hum,
Dancing meteors to the drum,
Jupiter spins a playful tale,
While Saturn's rings jingle and sail.

Cosmic jokes on every hue,
Stars share secrets just for two,
Alien giggles fill the air,
With every quip, we shed a care.

Galaxy's laughter, boosting spirits,
Stars and planets play their lyrics,
In a toast to silly quirks,
Life's bright punchlines, how it works!

Join the fun, and feel the glee,
In swirling whirlpools of esprit,
For in this cosmic dance, we find,
Laughter brightens hearts and minds.

Enchanted Skies

Under twinkling, mystic haze,
Whimsical wonders set ablaze,
Shooting stars with silly pranks,
Floating while the laughter tanks.

Dreamy clouds that giggle soft,
Spinning tales from dreams aloft,
Nebulas bursting with delight,
Crafting smiles on every flight.

Galactic goofiness takes hold,
In cosmic kitchens, laughter's bold,
Starry chefs whip up the fun,
Baking joy 'til day is done.

So let your spirit dance up high,
In these enchanted, glowing skies,
As playful echoes rule the night,
And fill your heart with purest light.

Astronauts of Joy

Floating high in spacesuits bright,
We're all clowns in starry night,
Rocket-fueled with laughter's roar,
Chasing giggles evermore.

Zipping past the planets' play,
Grins are strewn along the way,
With every flip, a jolly twirl,
The universe becomes our swirl.

Cosmic tickles tease our minds,
Orbiting joy, no one's blind,
From moonwalks to the asteroids,
Every leap, a burst of joys.

Hand in hand, we float and spin,
Through the vastness, we all grin,
In this laughter-filled expanse,
Together, let us take a chance.

Universe of Bliss

In a bubble bath of stars, we float,
Tickled by the comets' whirring note.
Planets dance with a silly spin,
While aliens giggle, wide-eyed with grin.

Space cows jump over the milky way,
Mooing jokes that brighten the day.
Wormholes twist in a playful chase,
As laughter echoes through time and space.

Asteroids tease with their zippy moves,
While rockets groove to interstellar grooves.
A fun fair on Saturn's rings so bright,
With shooting stars lighting up the night.

Each nebula whispers a joyous riddle,
As meteors play a musical fiddle.
In this realm where the silly are king,
Come join the party, let your heart sing!

Twinkling Cheer

Stars wear hats and twirl about,
Stellar giggles is what it's about.
Dancing moons in a quirky parade,
Neptune's pulling pranks, unafraid.

Spaceships playing tag with delight,
Chasing meteors, oh what a sight!
In this void, humor's our guide,
Laughter echoes on the cosmic tide.

Planets dressed in polka dots,
Join the fun, connect the knots.
Nebulas puffing like cotton candy,
In this playground, life is dandy.

Shooting stars with wild bold patterns,
Make wishes fly like happy lanterns.
In the vastness, joy takes flight,
Together we sparkle through the night!

Comet's Caress

Comets whirl in a gleeful dance,
With winks and nudges, they take a chance.
In perfect alignment, starlight winks,
While Jupiter's moon quietly thinks.

Zany rockets zoom with glee,
Finding lost socks, oh what a spree!
Across the black, we laugh and play,
In the cosmic café, all's okay.

Black holes whisper in riddle-filled tones,
Tickling space with giggly groans.
Zipping through time, we can't resist,
Breaking all rules just to coexist.

Supernovas burst with a glittery flair,
Filling the night with a delightful air.
In this realm where joy doesn't cease,
We twirl and whirl, finding our peace!

Interstellar Merriment

In a field of stars, we trip and tumble,
Giggling at quirks, making hearts humble.
Pulsars play peek-a-boo with delight,
As laughter rings out in the still of the night.

Astro-balloons float with a pop,
While saturnine jokes make us stop and drop.
The milky way serves cosmic ice cream,
In a swirl of flavors, we cheer and beam.

Cosmic puppies chase comet tails,
With wagging joy, they light up our trails.
In this playground where laughter is vast,
The future's bright, let's hold it fast!

Through cosmic fun, we'll boldly go,
With humorous tales that endlessly flow.
Embracing the quirkiness, we find our truth,
In the universe's play, we reclaim our youth!

Astral Amusement

Stars in the night, they wink and twirl,
Planets do cartwheels, a cosmic whirl.
Comets laugh out loud, trailing their tails,
While rockets do dances, floating like whales.

Frisky meteors bounce off the moon,
A playful ballet, in the quiet tune.
Aliens play tag with a gleeful cheer,
Bouncing off nebulae, oh what a sphere!

Cosmic jokes shared over stardust wine,
Laughter echoes wide across the divine.
Under the sun's gaze, they giggle and glide,
Through fields of starbursts, in joy they abide.

Saturn's rings spin tales, oddly sublime,
While singing black holes play games with time.
Twinkling stars chuckle as planets collide,
In this ludicrous realm, we all take a ride.

Elysian Echoes

In the realm of dreams, there's giggles and glee,
Galactic creatures, all playful as can be.
A comet rolls by, tripping on starry lace,
Unruly and jolly, it quickens its pace.

Cosmic clowns tumble through vibrant skies,
Juggling asteroids while crafting their pies.
Each laugh is a twinkle, each grin a delight,
Over cosmic highways, they frolic at night.

Lollipop planets spin round on a ride,
Chasing the moonbeams that glitter and glide.
Meteor showers rain giggles on Mars,
Creating a frolic beneath twinkling stars.

As the sun sets low, the moons start to play,
Pulling the galaxies into their sway.
With every echo, laughter fills the air,
In this comical cosmos, there's joy everywhere!

Beyond the Milky Smirk

Wobbling stars do the galaxy shimmy,
Dancing all night, oh isn't it whimsy?
Saturn spins tales, with rings full of cheer,
As Mars tells a joke that's fit for a sphere.

Asteroids roll in, making quite the fuss,
Their chuckles resound, creating a rush.
While Venus zips by in a sparkly dress,
Winking at Jupiter, who loves to impress.

Galaxies twirl in an endless embrace,
Hiccups and giggles fill up the space.
Each quasar a jester, shining so bright,
Lighting the cosmos with laughter at night.

Slapstick supernovas, loud bursts of fun,
Creating new worlds when their skits are done.
In this whimsical expanse, all worries are thin,
Welcome to the cosmos where we all wear a grin!

Jovial Junctures

Through swirling stardust, mischief unfolds,
As goofy green aliens share tales untold.
With laughter, they bounce on celestial beams,
Spinning their stories as bright as our dreams.

Silly suns giggle, igniting the skies,
With solar flares dancing, much to our surprise.
While planets play hopscotch, skipping along,
In this joyful expanse, there's never wrong.

Whimsical winks from the faraway stars,
A comical chorus that travels from Mars.
Clouds of confetti float gently around,
Creating a carnival in sight and sound.

Twilight arrives with a chuckle and grin,
As the universe winks, inviting us in.
In the orbit of laughter, we spin and we sway,
Together in this jest, where we frolic and play.

Twilight Tranquility

Balloons in space, they're floaty and bright,
  Wobbling around in the cosmic night.
  Aliens dancing with clueless style,
  Turning black holes into a giggling mile.

Stars with moustaches, twinkling with glee,
  Comets running races, just wait and see!
  Space cats juggling, what a sight to behold,
  Purring in rhythms of humor untold.

Cosmic bats flapping in glittery capes,
  Making up stories of fantastical shapes.
  Galactic playgrounds of laughter and cheer,
  Inviting all beings to join in the sphere.

Moonbeams are tickling, can you feel the fun?
  Chasing off shadows, they're on the run!
  In this twilight, where joy takes flight,
  The cosmos is laughing — oh, what a night!

Stardust Serenade

Whirling in circles, the planets do spin,
With a wink and a nod, let the laughter begin.
Dancing through stardust, with giggles galore,
Sassy little meteors tapping at the door.

Shooting stars play tag, zooming past the sun,
Crafting constellations, having way too much fun.
Each pinch of starlight, a chuckle on cue,
Ticklish comets with a shimmering view.

Asteroid dogs chase their tails in the dark,
Chuffing with joy, they light up the park.
Nebulae swirling in colors so bright,
Chortling together, a marvelous sight.

Planets crack jokes, oh what a delight,
Winking at Earth, 'you're quite a funny sight!'
In this dance of wonder, laughter's the key,
In the song of the cosmos, come laugh with me!

Luminous Laughter

Bright, giggling spheres floating high above,
Shooting out rays like a sun's warm love.
Marshmallow moons bounce in a playful spree,
Clouds made of candy: oh, can it be?

Stars cracking jokes tucked under their glow,
Poking fun at the planets below.
A merry little cluster with high-fives in tow,
Together they twinkle, steal the whole show.

Dizzy dandelions whisked into the fray,
Wishing on wishes that dance and sway.
Silly comet tails trailing sparkles so bright,
They twirl with the laughter of cosmic delight.

Halfway to Pluto, they throw a grand bash,
With giggles and grins, oh what a splash!
In this lighthearted realm, where whimsy finds worth,
Join in the laughter, it's all about mirth!

Ethereal Embrace

Bubbles of joy drift through the night sky,
Fluffy puffs of whimsey that float and fly.
Silly space critters bouncing on stars,
Trading high-fives while counting the Mars.

Tickling stardust with all of their might,
Sparks of laughter illuminating the night.
Invisible unicorns trot past the sun,
Cracking up clouds like they're having fun.

Galactic whispers of jokes never stale,
Each twinkle recorded in a cosmic tale.
Radiant rainbows curve over the tune,
As laughter erupts like a bright afternoon.

With hugs made of light, they gather in peace,
Sharing their quirks, pure joy will never cease.
In this ethereal realm, come join in the chime,
Where laughter's the rhythm, and joy's the prime!

www.ingramcontent.com/pod-product-compliance
Lightning Source LLC
Chambersburg PA
CBHW051642160426
43209CB00004B/763